Written by Susan Griffiths
Illustrated by Peter Townsend

Contents	Page
Chapter 1. *A hunting trip goes wrong*	4
Chapter 2. *A new, secret painting*	10
Chapter 3. *Very strange behaviour*	16
Chapter 4. *The village is saved*	24
Verse	32

Nelson
an International Thomson Publishing company I(T)P®

The Mammoth Hunters

With these characters ...

Muggs

Gert

Bogg

Sodds

Dubbo

"The thunderou

Setting the scene ...

Muggs is the worst mammoth hunter in the village—he'd rather spend time in his cave, painting pictures on the stone walls. But as time passes, even the best hunters cannot catch enough mammoths to keep the village from starving. Suddenly, while painting one day, Muggs has a crazy idea that might just work. He acts very strangely, and the villagers think he has gone mad ... until he reappears one night in great excitement!

"ootsteps of the mammoth
tormed closer and closer."

Chapter 1.

The huge, hairy mammoth raised its trunk and roared a bone-shattering roar. It stamped its front foot so hard that the snow-drifts in the trees crashed to the ground. It snorted and its breath gushed in clouds of icy steam. Then, just as Muggs had feared he would, the furious mammoth lowered its gleaming, razor-sharp tusks towards him. It began to charge.

"Oh, no," said Muggs, his heart pounding as panic set in. "Not again!"

He leapt to his feet, turned around and sprinted away. He knew that it was pointless. The mammoth was bigger, stronger and faster than him—and very, very angry.

In fact, as Muggs knew, few things made a mammoth angrier than a blunt stone arrow bouncing off its hairy bottom. Which was exactly what had just happened.

The thunderous footsteps of the mammoth stormed closer and closer, as Muggs frantically scampered over the icy ground. Although he tried to outrun the mammoth, the huge beast was gaining on him. He could almost feel its warm breath on his neck, and imagine the fury of its tiny, yellow eyes burning into his back.

Then, a second too late, Muggs noticed a tree root sticking out of the snow. His foot caught under the root, and he tripped head over heels and landed flat on his face in something warm and awful-smelling. He played dead. He didn't move a muscle. As the roar of the mammoth came closer and closer, the ground shook beneath him. Muggs waited for the sharp jab of the mammoth tusk in his back.

But the mammoth thundered straight past Muggs. The huge beast slowed down, and raised its giant, hairy head. It sniffed and snorted and shook its head from side to side. Muggs knew that mammoths had poor eyesight. He realised that the angry animal had lost the scent of one very scared human.

The mammoth stamped its feet again, snorted one more time, and stomped off. After a few minutes, Muggs stood up, wiping the greeny-brown muck out of his eyes.

"Mammoth dung," he spluttered and spat. "Muggs, the brave mammoth hunter, has avoided danger by hiding in mammoth dung!"

The pale sun was low in the sky as Muggs collected his few remaining arrows. Feeling dejected, he began to trudge home before the long Arctic night fell. As he walked, he tried to brush the mammoth dung off his skin and out of his hair, but it was no use. He smelt awful.

Finally, Muggs arrived at his village, exhausted. Smoke hung in the air around the tents made from mammoth skins and huge, curving mammoth tusks and bones. The other mammoth hunters were laughing and joking inside their tents. One of the villagers heard Muggs scuffing across the snow and poked his head out.

"Hello, Bogg," said Muggs flatly.

"No luck today, Muggs?" grinned Bogg. "Phew, you're a bit whiffy!"

Muggs shook his head, and entered his small tent. His sister Gert greeted him.

"Gert, I'm just not meant to be a mammoth hunter," blurted out Muggs. "I don't have the skill and the strength to outsmart the great mammoths."

"Maybe you're right," smiled Gert, sniffing the mammoth dung odour wafting from Muggs. "Maybe there are other things that you can do to help the village," she said, trying to encourage him.

Muggs and Gert shared a bowl of watery soup, made from left-over mammoth that the other villagers had caught and divided amongst everyone. The laughing of the other mammoth hunters grew louder.

"Poor, useless Muggs," they would say. "He's more interested in painting mammoths than catching them."

Chapter 2.

The next morning, Muggs looked at his arrows and shook his head. One disastrous hunting expedition in a week was more than he could bear. The smell of the mammoth dung lingered on his skin. Instead, he trudged down to the riverside. Behind a large, round boulder, was the entrance to a huge cave.

Inside the cave, Muggs waited for his eyes to adjust to the darkness. After a few minutes, he could see some familiar patterns on the walls. There, high on the right, was a collection of hand prints that he had been painting since he was a young boy. Below the hand prints, Muggs had drawn some animals: a herd of reindeer, a family of bears and a gang of angry mammoths.

But Muggs was not interested in the hand prints or the animal paintings anymore. For the last few weeks, he had been working on his new, secret painting.

Using black ash from the fire, red colouring from the soil, and green dyes he had squeezed out of plants and flowers, he was creating a huge painting of the land and the animals that surrounded his village. Little did he know that his picture story was going to become very important in the coming months.

The winter that year turned much colder than usual: the snow was deeper, the rivers froze over much earlier, and so did Bogg's beard. The long, dark nights seemed to go on forever. Even with three layers of mammoth skin blankets wrapped around their sleeping bodies, everyone shivered at night.

Every week, Bogg and the other mammoth hunters left the village in search of mammoths. Usually, there were so many mammoths, they could stand on a hilltop and spot them easily. They didn't have to hide or chase after them for very long. But they were becoming scarce.

A mammoth was big enough to feed the whole village for a week. Its hairy skin provided warm clothes and blankets for the freezing days and nights. The bones and tusks were used to build big, strong houses. The fat underneath the mammoths' skin could be burned in stone bowls to provide light and warmth. The village depended on mammoths for their survival.

But more and more, Bogg and the other hunters returned home with no mammoths.

"Those mammoths are becoming more scarce than sabre-tooth tigers," Bogg grumbled one day, as they trudged home. "Soon, we'll have to grow our own food and eat vegetables and fruit instead of mammoths!"

The other mammoth hunters were horrified at the thought of having to dig up the cold ground and plant vegetables. In comparison to mammoth hunting, it sounded like hard work!

"I'm only joking," grinned Bogg. "I'm sure the mammoths will return soon."

But the number of mammoths became fewer and fewer, and the villagers had to catch small snow rabbits and gather nuts from the forest to eat. The snow rabbits and nuts weren't as tasty as a great mammoth roasted over a roaring fire, but there was no choice.

During the morning, everyone in the village searched for food. Even Muggs was able to catch rabbits and gather nuts. Then, every afternoon, he walked down to his cave and continued painting.

He painted the hills and the river that snaked through the valley. He drew in the forest, using different marks for the various types of plants and trees. He added pictures of all the villagers and their houses. And he drew the snow rabbits and nuts that they had eaten for food.

After a long, cold month, when no-one had caught a single mammoth, Bogg summoned everyone in the village to a meeting.

"I'm tired of eating stringy little rabbits and chewy old nuts," he complained. Everyone gathered around him grunted in agreement.

"We need to capture a mammoth urgently," he said, rubbing his stomach. "Here's a plan!"

Chapter 3.

Bogg pointed to the most skillful mammoth hunter. "Dubbo, you must head towards the place where the sun rises." He pointed to another clever hunter. "Sodds, you will head towards the place where the sun sets. Muggs and I will remain in the middle. Hopefully, one of you will be able to chase a mammoth in our direction. Then we will capture it and have some decent food for a change!"

Muggs felt nervous. He didn't want an angry mammoth being chased in *his* direction. But he was ravenous, too, so he agreed with the plan.

Dubbo and Sodds set off in opposite directions. Muggs and Bogg waited between them, with their bows and freshly sharpened arrows and spears ready for action. For hours, nothing happened.

Then, just as the sun was overhead, they heard a rumbling noise and Sodds shouting in the distance. "Here comes dinner," said Bogg, grinning. "Make sure your aim is good!"

Suddenly, Muggs and Bogg saw what was making the rumbling sound. A huge mammoth was racing across the frozen ground towards them. Behind it, scrambling through the snow as fast as he could, Sodds was shouting and waving his arms around furiously.

Muggs trembled as the huge beast stampeded closer and closer. Then, just as he was trying to control his shaking hands to pull back his arrow, the mammoth skidded to a halt. It had spotted them!

Muggs looked to Bogg for instructions, but he was alarmed to see that even Bogg had a horrified look on his face.

"Oh-oh," said Bogg. "Now we're in trouble!"

The huge mammoth stamped its great hairy feet, and lowered its head. Gleaming sharp tusks glinted in the weak sunlight. "Phwww!" it snorted, and big white clouds of steam hung in the cold air. Hunting a mammoth that had seen you, and was *not* in a good mood, always ended in trouble.

"W-w-what sh-shall we do now?" stammered Muggs, as he stared at the massive mammoth.

There was no reply. He turned and saw Bogg scampering back to the village. Muggs turned to flee, too. But he was too late.

With a huge roar, the mammoth charged. The thunder of its feet on the ground grew louder and louder. Muggs looked around, desperately seeking a place to hide. He spotted a pile of old mammoth dung, heaped on the ground. With a sigh, he closed his eyes. He knew what he had to do.

That night, around the village fire, the villagers discussed how their plan had failed. Muggs sat alone, shivering on a log away from the fire. No-one could bear to sit next to him. Smelling of mammoth dung again, he was covered from head to foot in horrible clumps of brown dirt. He slunk off to wash in the icy river.

No-one could think of another plan. They all stared at the fire, feeling pangs of hunger as their empty stomachs rumbled. It was another cold, hungry night.

The next morning, Muggs returned to his cave. His stomach hurt. Gert had had nothing to put into her soup that morning. Neither did anybody else.

When Muggs looked at his painting, he decided to paint the failed mammoth hunt.

Once he drew in some trees and the angry mammoth, he coloured in the pictures with plant dyes.

Then, he stood back and studied his painting. As he tried to decide where to draw Bogg and himself, suddenly, he realised something very important.

If there had only been trees around the mammoth, it would have had no reason to become angry. Without him and Bogg in the painting, the mammoth would have been quiet and calm. And even Muggs knew that quiet and calm mammoths were easier to catch.

Muggs stared out the cave entrance toward the frozen river and the quiet forest. What a brainwave! He remembered that mammoths had terrible eyesight. His new plan sounded crazy— but he was hungry enough to try it.

Muggs ran out into the forest and collected twigs and leaves. Once he had stuffed them into his clothes and tied them around his arms and legs, he put more leaves into his long, dark hair. Then he scooped up a handful of mud, closed his eyes, and wiped it all over his face, arms and legs. Finally, he crept back to the village, hoping that no-one would see him.

Luckily, everyone was huddled inside their tents, trying to keep warm. Muggs sneaked around the outside of the village until he reached his tent. He quietly pulled back the flap.

Suddenly, he froze! The gleaming blade of a spear was pointing straight at him.

"Gert, it's me," whispered Muggs. Gert clutched the spear tightly, ready to throw it at the monster invading her tent.

"Muggs?" she asked in disbelief, lowering the spear. "Is that you?"

"Yes," replied Muggs, breathing a sigh of relief.

"I didn't know *what* was coming into our tent," said Gert, still trembling. "You look like a tree," she said. "Have you been tripping over in mammoth dung again?"

"No, but I might be soon," said Muggs, grinning as he grabbed his bow and arrows. "I'll see you later."

Muggs hurried out of the tent. Gert wanted Muggs to explain his strange behaviour, but he disappeared before she could ask.

"I think he's gone mad with hunger," she said to herself. "Poor Muggs."

Chapter 4.

Muggs was gone for hours and hours. As daylight slowly faded and the long night arrived, Gert started to feel really worried about her brother. First, he had appeared looking like some kind of walking tree, and then he had disappeared with his bow and arrows. And now, during the freezing night, he still had not returned. Gert hurried over to Bogg's tent.

"Bogg, I'm worried about Muggs," she explained in a worried voice. "He's been acting very strangely. And now he's disappeared." She told him about the afternoon's events.

Bogg agreed that it was very weird for someone to be walking around covered in mud, leaves and twigs. Even though Muggs had done some crazy things, this was the craziest. He called a meeting of the villagers. Everyone crowded into his tent, as he explained the problem.

"We have to go and search for poor, mad Muggs," he said. "He needs our help."

Everyone hurried back to their tents and returned to the meeting place with their spears, bows and arrows. They lit torches of wood to see by. The forest could be a dangerous place in the middle of the night.

Back at Bogg's tent, Bogg was giving instructions.

"Sodds, you and Guff head towards the river. Tubs, you and Dubbo head towards the hills. Gert, you and I will search around the cave."

"Eeeeek!" Sodds, who was standing on the outside of the group, gave a frightened shout. Everyone whirled around in horror. A terrifying forest monster had emerged from the darkness, and was running straight for them!

No-one had ever seen *anything* like the monster that was bearing down on them. It was shadowy and green, with leaves and branches waving from its body. It was making strange noises and panting loudly. Everyone grabbed their spears. Then Gert cried out.

"STOP! It's Muggs!"

And it was. He looked even worse than when she had last seen him. He was puffed, but his eyes were gleaming in the torchlight. He reached the group, and waved his leafy arms around.

"I need your help," said Muggs breathlessly.

Gert smiled kindly at her brother. "We know you do," she said softly. Everyone stared at Muggs and nodded in agreement. Then, just to confirm everyone's fears, he started to laugh.

"No, no," he said brightly. "There's nothing wrong with *me*!"

No-one was convinced.

"I need your help down there!" said Muggs, pointing back at the forest. "Quickly!"

Reluctantly, everyone followed Muggs. Bogg and Sodds rolled their eyes at each other. They walked through the dark forest, until they reached a large open field on the other side. In an instant, they realised what Muggs needed help with. They all stared in disbelief.

Chapter 5.

A huge mammoth, that would provide food, warmth and shelter for the hungry villagers, lay in the middle of the field.

"But how ...?" asked Bogg in amazement.

"My disguise, of course," replied Muggs, pointing at the leaves, twigs and mud that covered his body. "The mammoth didn't realise I was a human until it was too late," he said proudly.

Everyone stared at the mammoth, and then they stared at Muggs. He really was a genius, they thought. Then they all congratulated him and clapped and cheered. The worst mammoth hunter had saved their village.

The villagers skillfully carved up the mammoth, and carried the meat, skin, bones *and* their new hero, Muggs, back through the forest. Back at their village, they gathered around a roaring fire to roast mammoth steaks and re-enact Muggs' successful ambush.

The celebrations continued through the night, until everyone was tired, full and warm again. And from that day on, no-one laughed at Muggs again. Not even when, a year later, he came up with another crazy idea, after completing a new section of his cave painting.

"I've been thinking," he said. "It really would be very useful if we could plant some trees and vegetables close to our village. Then we wouldn't have to hunt through the forest every day. Maybe we'll get used to eating plants. We could call it a garden."

Everyone looked curious.

"Well," said Bogg, pushing his spear into the ground and turning over a lump of soil. "Let's give it a go. It might just work!"

"I've been thinking ..."

There once was a man in a cave,
Whose exploits were not very brave.
With one bright idea,
He conquered his fear,
And from hunger, his village was saved!